THE HEART OF A
SPARTAN

DONOVAN J. ROLLE SR.

Copyright © 2021 Donovan J. Rolle Sr.

All rights reserved. No part of this book may be reproduced, stored, or transmitted by any means—whether auditory, graphic, mechanical, or electronic—without written permission of the author, except in the case of brief excerpts used in critical articles and reviews. Unauthorized reproduction of any part of this work is illegal and is punishable by law.

ISBN: 978-1-7162-7952-2 (sc)
ISBN: 978-1-7162-7951-5 (e)

Library of Congress Control Number: 2021900262

Because of the dynamic nature of the Internet, any web addresses or links contained in this book may have changed since publication and may no longer be valid. The views expressed in this work are solely those of the author and do not necessarily reflect the views of the publisher, and the publisher hereby disclaims any responsibility for them.

Any people depicted in stock imagery provided by Getty Images are models, and such images are being used for illustrative purposes only.
Certain stock imagery © Getty Images.

Lulu Publishing Services rev. date: 03/25/2021

Dedicated to those who have decided to eliminate the following words from their minds:

No
Never
Can't
Quit
Defeat
_____
_____
_____

*Fill in the blanks.

When it is obvious that the goals cannot be reached,
don't adjust the goals, adjust the action steps.

—Confucius

Contents

Acknowledgments xi
Foreword xv

Chapter 1	I Am Jay	1
Chapter 2	Your Mind Is Your Only Limit	4
Chapter 3	Goal Setting	7
Chapter 4	The Road to Recovery	10
Chapter 5	Get Ya Mind Right	13
Chapter 6	Consistency or Silence	16
Chapter 7	Trust the Process	19
Chapter 8	But Did You Die?	22
Chapter 9	Find Your Why	25
Chapter 10	Exceeding Expectations	30
Chapter 11	Pain over Regret	34
Chapter 12	This Is Sparta	37
Chapter 13	The Heart of a Spartan	42
Chapter 14	Jay All Day	45
Chapter 15	Proper Training	48
Chapter 16	Family First	52
Chapter 17	Leaving a Legacy	54

Acknowledgments

I knew I needed to maximize my time of solitude. I knew that there had to be others before me who had gone through and others after me who would be going through what lay before me post-surgery. I believed that someone somewhere at some time would benefit from the path that was thrust upon me. I understood that the lessons learned from the injury and the journey to recovery would be not only lessons to aid others in overcoming their injuries but a metaphor for life through which we all can overcome various physical and mental obstacles we'll face.

My biggest challenge was that I did not know how to start this project. I reached out to a few individuals, all of whom were excited about the idea as well as their involvement. But as life would have it, they fell through. One day, I reached out to another individual for help in finding someone who would be able to assist and also willing to take on the task.

In my isolation, I had time to reflect, and the vision became so clear. I quickly called that individual back and said, "Bey, you don't want to do dis, eh, or are you afraid to be great?" Then, with laugher of course, he replied, "I was just thinking the same thing." This book is a product of that phone call.

Due to his humble heart, he would claim that he only captured my words. This project could not have been done without the passion, commitment, and excellence he brought to it. I would not have been able to finish if he had not started. So, I would like to publicly acknowledge and say thank you to:

Rodney D. Bain Jr.

I would also like to thank two individuals who, through their collaborative efforts, have ensured that the respective book covers of not only this project but my first project, as well as upcoming projects encapsulate the book content and titles; even though I was unable to verbalize what I actually wanted (LOL), they get me.

A *big* thank-you to the team at Eye Candy Makeup Store Bahamas, and in particular Italia, for their cosmetic artwork and costuming. Italia said, "Jay, when you are ready, just let me know, and I'll sort that out." Years later, I gave her a call, and so said, so done. Thank you.

Kovah from KovahDuncombe Photography is the man behind the camera. Time after time, I make his job harder than it has to be. I clearly have a problem with following directions. There was never a time I needed his services and he wasn't there. Thank you.

Foreword

The Heart of a Spartan by Donovan J. Rolle Sr. is filled with lessons and examples of times when the writer faced difficulties, setbacks, and disappointments and how he overcame them. The stories resonate with the reader, and the messages of hope and motivation and the challenge for readers to "get your mind right" inspire the reader to look past current situations and to take steps to achieve their dreams and push past their comfort zones.

I found the book to be well thought out and well written. The author's use of personal stories as well as the stories of others who've pushed past limitations makes the book relatable to everyone. *The Heart of a Spartan* spoke directly to me. I was captivated by the book and found it difficult to put down.

If you are serious about achieving your goals and dreams, this book provides many keys to help you get there. It provides a guide for the reader to use to create their plan.

Duquesa D. Dean

CHAPTER 1

I Am Jay

There is nothing I cannot do physically. To me, it is never a matter of whether I will finish; it is only a matter of how much time it will take me to finish. I have found that this leads me to be competitive in anything I undertake. Whether it is due to nature or nurture, competition is in my blood.

My thirst for competition led me to enter the Spartan Race. The Spartan Race is a series of obstacle-course races of varying distances with varying numbers of obstacles over rugged terrain that reward participants with thirty burpees for failing to complete an obstacle. I had never done anything like it before, but I knew I could do it simply because there is nothing I physically cannot do. If another human being can do it, then I know I can do it. Give me ample training, sufficient time, and the proper parameters, and I will accomplish the task. I firmly believe that if you put your best foot forward, give maximum effort, and do not give up, there are few things that you cannot conquer.

People often describe me as *competitive*, *driven*, or *confident*. I believe this is due to my demeanor in competition. I truly believe that if someone else can do it, then I can do it as well. I may have to train harder, longer, or with more energy, but I can definitely do it. However, if I were to describe myself, I would use *introvert*, *family oriented*, and *driven*.

Despite what people may believe, I prefer to be away from crowds. I do not get affirmation from the outside. I am sure about who I am and comfortable in my skin. I feel that if you are truly self-aware, then you will not be swayed by others' interpretations of you. Family is very important to me. My children, my parents, and my close circle are the reason behind it all. I attribute my driven nature to my family.

I grew up in an environment where competition was encouraged. Both my parents competed in athletic arenas, and both had a thirst for winning. It was not enough to compete; winning was, and is, important. However, the greatest victory one can ever experience is conquering self-doubt and focusing one's mind. With parents like mine, it was hard to be less than. It was not nature, but a great deal was nurture. They did not shun losing, nor did they overemphasize winning. They led by their actions. I admire them in so many ways. I am constantly grateful for what they directly or indirectly poured into me, making me who I am. I aspire to be like them, accomplish what they have done, and leave my imprint on the world as they left theirs on my life.

Building on this foundation, I found fitness a natural transition. I went from transforming my own body to assisting others to realize their body goals. Our constant mantras are "Get ya mind right" and "Consistency or silence." Either you are consistent with your goals or—to put it bluntly—you simply shut up about them. I do not believe in words without actions. Our actions will always speak louder than our words. I am by nature animated when I speak, but I ensure my actions, my deeds, and my dedication precede, exceed, and represent my words very well.

Fitness doesn't happen by accident; it's an intentional decision to consistently be better.
—Donovan J. Rolle Sr.

I am fairly active in organizations outside work. I enjoy service in many forms and giving back where I can. Fitness and competition have been two of my greatest interests. Like my parents, I have participated in countless competitions and won many. From competitions to friendlies, walkathons to triathlons, fitness training to gym reps, there are not many events that

I have passed up. I am now to the point where I am no longer looking to win; I am looking to expand my limitations. I now look for events that I have to train harder and longer for.

In 2017, my new challenge was the Spartan Trifecta. To obtain this accolade, one must complete the Spartan Sprint, the Spartan Super, and the Spartan Beast within the same calendar year. I had completed the Spartan Sprint, a three- to five-mile race with twenty to twenty-five obstacles, and the Spartan Super, an eight- to ten-mile race with twenty-five to thirty obstacles. Remaining was the Spartan Beast. The Spartan Beast is a twelve- to fourteen-mile race with thirty to thirty-five obstacles.

Months before the Spartan Beast, I encountered a delay—not a stoppage, just a delay. The unexpected happened. Something that I had never experienced. Something that may have slowed me but did not stop me.

CHAPTER 2

Your Mind Is Your Only Limit

It was Sunday, and I was at my fraternity's obstacle course race. I had done obstacle courses as well as races before, so why would this be a challenge? There I was, on the last leg of the final event for the day. Looking at the people running with me, I began to size them up. Although I was 39, I knew if I was strategic that I could compete with these younger members who were in their 20s. So, there I was, waiting, ready.

Boom! I got the baton, and I was off, up and over the ten-foot inclined wall. I ran about thirty meters on the sand, under an obstacle, over another, high knees through some tires, and over a four-foot wall. And then, there was the last obstacle—a six-foot inclined wall. Up to that time, I had never had a major injury before. But as soon as I began to climb the wall, I knew that something was wrong.

I felt the snap and heard it in surround sound simultaneously. I had the presence of mind to gently usher myself down the wall. I felt pain in my leg immediately, but I dared not look down to face reality. In fact, I pulled my shirt over my face and motioned for help. All I remember thinking was *Where is my knee?* As people rushed over to see what was wrong, I repeatedly asked the same question: "Where is my knee!" In my mind, my knee had done a 180.

Now lying on the ground, those who were there to help assured me that my knee was where it should be. Not believing them, and thinking that they just did not want to alarm me about the severity of my injury, I asked them to touch my knee so that I could confirm for myself that it was where it should be. I was too fearful to face what I thought was a misplaced kneecap.

The pain was indescribable. But honestly, I do not know what hurt more, hurting my knee or not finishing the race. Actually, the knee pain did more physical damage, but not finishing the race did more to me mentally. That is because up until then, there had been no race I could not finish. The only obstacle for me to overcome was time, not completion. But God has a plan for it all. He uses every situation to help guide us closer to Him and our purpose. And this was no different.

Well, in my mind, the knee had clearly shifted and then snapped back into place. Therefore, I was okay, with some slight discomfort of course. I was able to put light pressure on the knee and walk without assistance. I was under the impression that the injury was not that bad as long as I was able to put pressure on it, drive myself home, ice it, and rest. Maybe pride kept me going, or maybe my lack of experience with a major injury had me confused. Or plain stubbornness could have been why I saw no need to go to the hospital. But with family and friends like mine, I was going to the hospital whether I liked it or not.

When I got to the hospital, I expected the staff to tell me I had a simple sprain that would take a week or two to heal. I thought I would probably just need to ice it and rest it, and then, I would be in good shape. But by the tone of the conversation, I knew the doctor had other plans. Major damage had been done. Surgery was required. I had popped my quadriceps's tendon, apparently a common injury for middle-aged men. Not only was surgery required, but I had to go through rehabilitation after the recovery time—both things that I had no issues with. But then, the doctor told me the recovery time was six weeks! Before the start of rehabilitation, I would be immobile for six weeks! That news was more devastating than the injury.

After processing what the doctor had said, I concluded that it would take me less time to recover than the average six-week recovery time. I do not train like the average person, I do not exercise like the average person, and I do not treat my body like the average person. Therefore, I should not recover like the average person. And I did not expect to recover like the average person not just because I needed to be back at 100 percent for the Spartan Beast but because there is nothing I physically cannot do.

The surgery was a success. Now, it was recovery time. I tried to avoid being dependent on pain medication, but the pain was calling for it. I somehow managed the pain without medication from the third day after the surgery on, but the night of the surgery was a different story. Being in the hospital bed was just as painful as waiting for the pain medication to kick in. As this was my first major surgery, I had never had a prolonged hospital stay before. Now, to think of it, I had never been immobile that long before. I had had injuries in the past, but I had not been anchored to a bed as I was in the hospital. I do not know which was more difficult—the pain in my leg or my inability to walk around of my own will.

The support was great. My wife and family ensured I was well taken care of. The hospital staff was responsive. I just grew stir-crazy. Boredom was strong, and my mind wandered about how quickly I could recover and what all I needed to do. *Who do I need to see? Where do I need to go? And what do I need to do?* All those thoughts related to after I got out of this hospital and rested six weeks before the rehab.

**If you focus on what's behind,
you won't see what's ahead.
—Auguste Gusteau**

An important thing I keep in mind is to not live in the past. Yes, this was my first injury; yes, it was a major one; and yes, it was a hindrance, but it was not a roadblock. I cannot allow the fear of reinjuring myself to prevent me from growing and progressing. For many athletes who undergo a major injury, recovery is just as much mental as it is physical. The fear of reinjuring oneself, not recovering fully, or not being able to function in the same manner is present. But the important thing is to overcome that fear. You must overcome the shadow of past failures in order to enjoy the glory of future successes. Did the injury slow me down? Yes. Would it stop me? No. The injury simply resulted in a detour on the road to Sparta, and that detour took me straight to rehab.

CHAPTER 3

Goal Setting

I understand the importance of setting goals, so just three days after my surgery, I signed up for the Spartan Beast using the goal-setting SMART acronym.

- Specific—Spartan Trifecta
- Measurable—Spartan Beast
- Achievable—For sure
- Realistic—Apparently only to me
- Timely—December 9, 2017

A goal without a plan is just a wish.
—Antoine de Saint-Exupéry

Many of us meander through life wishing and hoping for things, just keeping the faith and dreaming of a better life. While I'm a firm believer in the concept of visualization, I more firmly believe in the Bible verse James 2:17. I understand that some improvements take small steps while others require a complete paradigm shift; regardless of the action steps, we will never attain a goal without consistent effort. I'm not one to put forth some effort and hope for the best. I set the goal and put in the work.

If you do not set goals, you will succeed at nothing; well, you'll excel at mediocrity—at best.

I often wonder why many individuals don't attain any of their goals and a small group of individuals often attain many of their goals. Is the difference effort? Are those who attain their goals setting the bar too low? Or are those who don't reach the mountaintop climbing someone else's mountain? Are you climbing the mountain of an engineer when you should be on a musician's mountain? Are you climbing the lawyer mountain when you should be climbing the artist mountain? Or are you climbing the mountain of the latest fad or the mountain of the career that looks good on someone you admire when you should be climbing the follow-your-dreams mountain?

Many of us fail at our goals because they are not our goals at all; they're our parents' goals, society's goals, or our friends' goals. We are so afraid to let our light shine that we hide our own goals, our passions, and our destiny deep down inside so they are now unknown to us. So before we can be SMART about our goals, we need to ensure that our goals are truly ours, and then, we must commit ourselves to the actions—slow although they may sometimes be—that will get us the results we so desire. No matter how small the steps, no matter how slow the pace, stay the course and win your race.

When setting goals, you must be mindful of goal killers. You must recognize procrastination disguised as the "planning process," lack of commitment to complete a task disguised as a break. With the setting, the planning, and the analyzing of goals, you will actually be your own biggest obstacle. You may allow doubt to set in. You may lack belief. You may lack the motivation to start, not to mention the motivation to finish. I think all of this is due to fear—fear of not being accepted, fear of failing, fear of disappointing yourself or others, fear of proving the naysayers right. But you need to grab hold of that fear because it isn't real. Fear is a taught emotion. The more you choke the life out of fear, the more you give your life to your dreams and goals. The more you face your fear, the more life itself will be revealed to you. Ignore it, face it, attack it, meditate on it, dance with it, talk to it; just do whatever it takes to deal with the illusion of fear.

> **Fear, to a great extent, is born of
> a story we tell ourselves.**
> —Cheryl Strayed

Set yourself up for the win. It's your race. You are the commissioner, the president, the CEO; you are the chairperson of the rules committee. Tilt the scales in your favor—rig the game and win. Set up the small wins to snowball the momentum for the big win. I had no idea whether my surgery had truly been a success. I had no idea how or if my body would ultimately respond positively to the procedure. I did not know the length of my rehab, nor what the rehab would entail. The only thing I knew was that I had set a goal and I was willing and prepared to put in the work to reach that goal.

> **Begin with the end in mind.**
> —Stephen Covey

CHAPTER 4

The Road to Recovery

Before rehab, there was the recovery. I was able to rest during this time. I had always been active; to be immobilized was something I was not accustomed to. I had to rest for about five weeks before I was cleared to start rehab. I committed that this injury would only slow me, not stop me. Stopping was not something I was willing to accept. The human body should always be in motion, and I was not willing to accept this non-active lifestyle. So, I counted down the days. In retrospect, five weeks felt like five months, but at the same time, it felt like five days to see where my progress is now. That taught me that the thing that seemed so dire and imposing during that time would be insignificant in hindsight.

I do not think I was your average patient when it came to physiotherapy. Before I started rehab, I knew that I would exceed the average expectation of six to eight weeks' recovery time. I knew my recovery would not be like the average person's because prior to the injury, I did not train like the average person, I did not eat like the average person, and I did not think like the average person. However, if you were to ask my physiotherapist, at day one, I was pretty average.

I had the regular questions and concerns anyone would have if they suffered an injury. *How long will it take to heal? How long will it be until I can be active again? Will there be any long-term constraints?* However, despite the questions about my body, my mind was ready to recover. I have learned that whatever you set your mind to; your body will follow. My mind was focused on recovery, so my body would follow.

Rehab became a new frontier for me to conquer. Getting back to where I needed to be in the time I needed to do it was a next mountain to overcome. A few people doubted this was something that I could do, but this was another opportunity to demonstrate my mental toughness and drive. Mentality is important to success. Once you can visualize your success, your body will follow. Battles are won and lost in the mind.

The hardest thing about rehab is the wait and anticipation of it. Rehab usually focuses on one muscle at a time, one task at a time, one small thing at a time. This actually was a huge life lesson for me. Rehab was never about just the rehabilitation session itself. I always had some preparation to do before and some work to do afterward. These tasks are what determine success. Yes, running miles is important, and lifting is vital, but rest is key, recovery is key, and stabilization is key.

It is like the human body; if you overdevelop the biceps without paying attention to the triceps, then you will be in trouble. The biceps are the sexy muscles, whereas the triceps make up about 75 percent of your arm. If you are not ready to do the extra things, focus on developing the support system, or rest as need be, you will get yourself into trouble. It is important to do the things that others do not see, to get you where you need to be. And I needed to be in rehab.

> **Success in life is founded upon attention to the small things rather than to the large things.**
> —Booker T. Washington

I never would have believed that a simple thing like flexing my muscle could be so hard, but rehab reminded me of the importance of going the extra mile. Rehab also taught me that I have to trust the process. The doctor had said the surgery was successful; the physiotherapist said the leg looked good. Now, it was time for me to put in the work so I could put in the work later.

Life is not just about accomplishing the grand-scale events. Life is made up of many small races that we must complete in order to get to the next level, the next chapter, or, in my case, the next competition. It is in these seemingly small moments that we realize our boundaries and then push beyond those boundaries. Because I knew what it was for me to be at 100 percent, I created a tangible rehab goal to aim for. Like with most things in my life, I did not want to merely make it to the finish line of rehab; I wanted to run through the tape at the rehab finish line.

I accepted that rehab was painful; I accepted that rehab was difficult. But ultimately, I accepted rehab as part of the plan. In order for me to attain my goal, I had to go through this difficulty, and I was not ready to let a setback delay my goal. If others could overcome similar injuries, why couldn't I? I wanted to be an example of success for someone. I wanted people to see me overcome my difficulty and be strengthened to overcome their issues. The longer we take to complete a race or reach our goals, the longer it will take for someone to be inspired and then motivated to start reaching their own goals.

I had to face a lot coming through this journey, a lot of sacrifices, difficulties, challenges, and injuries.
—Gabby Douglas

In life, some obstacle to accomplishing your goals will be placed in your path. Some roadblock, some deterrent, or something else will cause you to question whether you really want the goal. What I learned is that the race is about not how many obstacles are in an athlete's path but how skilled, resilient, and determined the athlete is in completing the course. Life is the same way. It is about not the issues you face but how you decide to face the issues.

Once you conquer a mountain, it diminishes the fear of the climb. But simply having confirmation of your ability to gain success does not make the climb less arduous or the path less treacherous; it simply makes the journey more worthwhile. This injury reminded me that expectations do not always equal reality and that to truly be able to accomplish a task, you have to prepare yourself for it both mentally and physically.

CHAPTER 5

Get Ya Mind Right

To some, "get ya mind right" may sound like a cliché fitness line. But to me, it is a way of life. Once you have the right thinking, your body and goals align. Progress starts with the head, and fitness and wellness are no different. There is little to no chance of success if the body moves independently and in opposition with the head. This can be seen in organizations, in countries, and most important in us. If we are not convinced that a new diet or exercise will benefit us, then we will not see results. This is due to our body's lack of action and our low level of mental engagement. The same works in reverse. Many people who subscribe to new weight-loss crazes see tremendous results due to their beliefs. Their mentality fuels the extra reps, fuels the extra miles, and turns away the extra helping of food. Success begins and ends in the mind.

**When there is no enemy within,
the enemies outside cannot hurt you.
—African proverb**

Self-motivation is the cornerstone of success, whereas self-sabotage is the finishing blow for every failure. Doubt starts to set in, and then we set ourselves up for failure. We brace for it by stopping the things necessary for us to succeed; that way, when we fail, we have reasons (more like excuses) to look at in order to justify our state of mediocrity. We start to move the goalpost not because of some self-actualization, some new information, or some external factor totally beyond our control. No, no, no, this new positioning is internally driven so that we can sleep better—feel better when we tell the story of why this didn't happen or how we were so ready for that thing but "life" had different plans for us (more likely, we had different plans for us).

Do we succeed at everything we do every time we do it? Of course not. Do we always put forth maximum effort in our preparation and execution? Of course not. I guess the point that I am trying to make is if we focus on the goals that we set for ourselves and go after them within the parameters of our respective lives with no excuses and no intentional self-inflicted land mines, we'll become more successful at life and future endeavors whether or not we arrive at the specific goalpost at its original location.

Doubt kills more dreams than failure ever will.
—Suzy Kassem

I'm not devoid of these feelings, thoughts, actions, and friendly fires. Two weeks out from the event, guess what I did for a few days—eat more and work out less. When I did drag myself to train, I did it with less intensity. I just went through the motions, justifying my actions with the thought that doing something is better than doing nothing, which is true. But greatness is achieved by doing small things well; there's nothing great about a half-assed workout.

Here's another thought I had at the time: *I'm tapering for the event.* Ha! Tapering is reserved for the conditioned and the prepared. I even convinced myself that I was just too tired to work out, but instead of not working out, I thought, *I'll take a power nap and go to the gym later.* Yeah right; as expected, I had a power *sleep*, not a power nap. *So now, I'm up at an ungodly late hour energized and ready to work out. But sadly, the gym is closed. Ah well, there's always tomorrow. But wait, I have bands, medicine balls, battle ropes, weights, kettlebells, a pull-up bar, TRX bands, and other gadgets. I can get a workout at home. But wait, they're outside, and the alarm is on. But wait, I know an array of body-weight exercises that I can do inside. Hmm … I'll just work extra hard tomorrow 'cause it's too late to wake up my family with all that jumping up and down and the noise.* Yes, my family who can sleep through a hurricane—true story. *But wait, since I'm driven, I have to make the best of this situation. Eureka! I'll have a light beer tonight instead of a normal one. Gotta watch those empty calories.*

That's just a few hours in one day that I allowed the mediocrity monster to acquire multiple victories so I might have a "reason" (excuse) for not completing the event. *Well, we know that's not going to happen. My Ghostbuster proton pack is arriving tomorrow to lay waste to that mediocrity monster.*

Fall down seven times, get up eight.
—Japanese proverb

CHAPTER 6

Consistency or Silence

The Oxford Advanced Learner's Dictionary defines *consistency* as the quality of always behaving in the same way or of having the same opinions, standards, etcetera. Think of how many things failed simply because they were not done with enough repetition and consistency. Just because something was not done right after the first attempt does not make it a failure. Through consistency, we create growth. We develop by repeating tasks and eventually mastering them. Once we master a task, we move on to another and then another. But in order to be masters of successes, we must first master ourselves. Things like discipline, drive, and dedication are products of an internal drive for excellence.

> Success isn't always about greatness. It's about consistency. Consistent hard work leads to success. Greatness will come.
> —Dwayne Johnson

There are no cheat codes to success. Hard work still is the pillar of success. Whether professional, physical, or relational, success is based on doing the small things consistently. We tend to only want to hit the home run or make the game-winning shot. However, many hours of work go into making those key moments possible. Do not allow the glitz and glamour of the mountaintop to cause you to take the climb for granted. It is those small steps that will make or break you during the climb. Are you learning on the way to the top? Are you making the best of the pitfalls that you encounter along the way? Or are you just so focused on the top that you do not appreciate how far you have climbed?

We tend to take the distractions, difficulties, and discouragements that flank the road to success for granted. There will be challenges, there will be naysayers, and there will be fatigue, but all those things are meant for you to overcome, not for you to be overwhelmed by. You cannot complain about the challenges if you are not doing what you need to do to overcome them. I cannot complain about race day if I know I slacked off in my workouts.

For me, rehab reinforced the importance of the small tasks. The few hours I spent in rehab were not the entirety of my rehabilitation. The warm-ups, the warm-downs, the stretches, the massages, the weight training, the icing—all those things and more made up my rehabilitation. If I slacked off in preparation, that made my session that much more difficult. Who am I to complain if I know I did not consistently prepare for the moment?

I have found that life is the same way. We have a few large moments that tend to define major milestones in our lives, and a great deal of smaller moments prepares us for each major event. Rarely are we placed in a situation that we are totally unprepared for. Life has a way of qualifying us for the next level before we reach the destination. The difficulties, distractions, and discouragements are training tools to prepare us for a major moment. However, if we lose sight of what our goals are, we will become lost in the challenges.

> **It's not what we do once in a while that shapes our lives. It's what we do consistently.**
> **—Anthony Robbins**

Now, the question is, What are you consistently doing? People say they try and try yet yield no results. But are you being honest with yourself?

Are you truly being disciplined, setting your goals, and working diligently toward them? Or, are you doing the bare minimum, or just enough to be noticed? What defines your journey are those things you consistently do when no one is watching. There are people who work only to be seen. Whenever their boss is not around, they do not put in an ounce of effort, but when the boss is there, it is showtime. In contrast, there are those persons who consistently work regardless of who is watching.

Do not be a talker. Be a doer. If you want a better life, create one. If you want to lose weight, make better food choices, and exercise. If you want more money, that may require a career change. No one is saying it will be easy, but it is not impossible.

Imagine you and two colleagues are climbing the same mountain of success. One of your companions is diligent, sure-footed, and focused, whereas the other is lazy, complains often, and is misguided. Who do you think will reach the top first and be more beneficial to your journey, and who will probably not see the mountaintop and potentially trip others along the way? Now, which one of these climbers are you? Are you sure-footed, or are you misguided? Are you a complainer, or are you a doer? Are you disciplined, or are you impulsive?

The climb will be difficult but not impossible. You can vent your frustrations, but do not become discouraged. You can rest, but do not stop. Consistency is key. So is silence. Either put in the work with the small, ugly, boring tasks to get to your big, glorious, rewarding mountaintop, or shut up about never reaching your goal and stop discouraging others who are on their way up the mountain. You decide.

**The world needs dreamers and the
world needs doers, but above all,
the world needs dreamers who do.**
—Sarah Ban Breathnach

CHAPTER 7

Trust the Process

Imagine you are preparing for a race. Your goal is to finish this race within ten minutes. You have prepared all you can for completing the goal within this set time. Now, you realize that circumstances have changed. What you thought would be a simple race has proven to be more challenging before you start. You have been thrown a curveball that you did not prepare for. But you still need to finish the race. How do you deal? How do you now refocus your mind to ensure you can still complete the race in the way that you originally planned?

What if I told you all the twists, disappointments, and unexpected changes are part of the process to prepare you for the race? This is the thought I had during rehab. I had a goal in mind. This goal was time sensitive. If I missed the window, I would have to start over from the beginning next year. The third and final leg of the race was only a few months away. If I did not recover in time, I would have to redo the first two races just to get back to this point.

I could not afford to stop. I could not afford to give up. But I could not help but think to myself, *Why did this injury happen? Why do we seemingly always experience setbacks at the worst times? Either things are going really good and there is a bump that slows us, or things are going really bad and there is a bump that further delays us.* Rarely are we prepared for a challenge when it comes; it feels as if challenges come when our guard is down. I had never had a major injury prior to this, the timing was not the best, and I did not understand why it happened.

> **When the student is ready, the teacher will appear.**
> **—Buddha**

The process is our teacher in life. We can see it as a necessary set of circumstances that help shape us for our goal. It prepares us for the thing we are seeking. Even if the preparation process proves to be painful, trying, and seemingly endless, we must trust that it serves a greater purpose. Ultimately, the process teaches us who we are able to become. In this process, we are shaped and molded to become greater versions of ourselves. The process is meant not to stop us but to teach us.

Looking in from the outside, people saw my injury as a reason to not pursue any more athletic events for the year and to give up on my goal of completing the Spartan Trifecta. However, I saw this injury as a reminder of the need to focus my mind, the importance of the little things, and the limitations of my body.

Many things I was experiencing were reminders of things I had learned in the past. From my years of competition, I had always known the importance of having good recovery habits and executing the small tasks. With this injury, I was able to refocus and realign my mind with this idea. My immobility provided a great deal of time to reflect. It also allowed me to assess my journey thus far: *I am far from where I need to be, but I can appreciate the process thus far.* Looking back down the mountain, I realized that I had overcome many tribulations and had claimed many victories on my way there. Not that self-confidence or self-motivation was an issue, but it is good to often remind yourself of who you are.

I also gained greater appreciation for the small tasks that help us get to where we want to be. This was bigger than physical recovery for me. The follow-up conversations, random phone calls, and spontaneous breakfasts are what keep life exciting and in perspective.

Too often, we fall into a rut and become content with what life throws at us, and we forget that we are active participants in this walk as well. Consistency is not the same as complacency. Consistency is doing the small things to get to your goals. Complacency is not caring whether you achieve your goals. If you ever forget the difference between consistency and complacency, life has a way of placing tribulations along your path to help you remember.

> **Transformation is a process, and as life happens there are tons of ups and downs. It's a journey of discovery—there are moments on mountaintops and moments in deep valleys of despair.**
> **—Rick Warren**

Whether it involves your mind, your body, or your life, the process of transformation is an uncomfortable one. Like our muscles, we are torn down to get built up stronger and more durable. We must remember that the goals we set and the dreams we put out there are being heard and we are being prepared for the mountaintops. Unfortunately, for every mountaintop, there are valley lows. However, our travels through the valley are what prepare us for the mountaintop experience. We just need to trust the transforming, qualifying, and strengthening process that prepares us for those mountaintops.

Would I have liked to not have to undergo surgery in order to remember the core values of rest, reflection, and focus? Most definitely! Would it have been as effective if I did not go through what I went through in the manner that I did? I will never know. What I do know, however, is that after all the negative experiences I faced and survived in the past, I am stronger and wiser. Moving forward, I must continue to trust the process and know that I will accomplish all I set my mind to.

> **However long the night, the dawn will break.**
> **—African proverb**

CHAPTER 8

But Did You Die?

If another human being can do something, then why should you not be able to do it? Your only question should be "How long will it take me, or how much training do I need?" We tend to undersell ourselves when something is hard or when it takes more effort than we are comfortable giving. We always think our best is our best until we surpass our best. This is why exposure is vital for growth.

If I see someone completing a task I have never done, I accept it as a challenge, not because I have a competitive nature but simply because I want to push my limitations. We tend to expand within the boundaries of our vision. Therefore, in order to grow, we need to elevate our vision. Is your lack of progress due to your efforts or due to your goals? Is your lack of breakthrough due to your pushing in the wrong direction? Maybe it is time for you to start exposing yourself to examples of greatness so you can map out your success.

We live in the age of instant information. Whether through books, blogs, or videos, find someone in a similar situation who overcame obstacles similar to yours. Many times, we fear jumping not because of the fall but because of the unknown outcome. You may hurt yourself, you may die, or you may also survive and adapt. You will never know unless you jump. If you choose to stay, you can be sure that you will not be challenged, you will not be fulfilled, and you will either develop regret for what could have been or doubt your abilities.

Failure is not the end. It is said that it is better to try and fail than to never try at all. My stance is to look at the worst-possible outcome of a scenario, which is usually death. If you did not die at the end of an experience, then you won, because I guarantee you learned something from that experience. Is this an extreme view? Maybe. But if you look at life in this way, everything short of death is a lesson that can be applied to future situations. The idea of failure is a misconception shared by the masses. We do not fail; instead, we learn, we grow, we adapt. In order to appreciate the ability to convert a loss to a win, you must expose yourself to people who have done it in the past. Use their experiences as road maps to your personal success, and become a success story for others.

Expose yourself to your deepest fear; after that, fear has no power, and the fear of freedom shrinks and vanishes. You are free.
—Jim Morrison

We are prisoners to our success, and our greatness is held captive by the limitations on our minds. Prior to 1954, a four-minute mile was unheard of. The experts of the time deemed it impossible. They said that the human body could not travel at the speed nor sustain the speed needed to run a mile in under four minutes. On May 6, 1954, at Oxford University's Iffley Road track, Roger Bannister, a man from Harrow, England, ran a mile in 3:59.4 minutes. Two months later, Bannister and another runner ran the distance in under four minutes. Ten years later, a high school runner, Jim Ryun, ran it in 3:59.0 minutes as a junior and then in 3:55.3 minutes as a senior. What was deemed impossible to accomplish more than sixty years ago is now the standard in the sport. Now, the question is this: Did Bannister's four-minute mile prove to the world that it was possible, thus allowing others to believe and break through, or would have the others broken though when they did, regardless of Bannister's accomplishment?

What is your four-minute mile? What is that thing that previous generations deemed impossible but your spirit is telling you to try? Are you willing to be the one to breakthrough so others can follow, or will you stand in the way of greatness? I am sure Bannister had many detractors to his success, along with many failures along the way, but he did not give up. He kept pushing and kept striving. Even after completing his first four-minute mile, he did not stop racing, because he had a goal beyond running a four-minute mile. His goal was to be the best runner he could be; he just so happened to accomplish the feat of being the first athlete to complete the four-minute mile. As for me, beyond finishing the Spartan Beast or a triathlon or any other competition along the way, I want to be the best version of myself I can be all day every day. If it comes with accolades and recognition, then so be it.

My greatest competition is myself. I know my limitations, and I challenge them often. If I prepare adequately, then I will succeed. If I cheat my preparation, then I will fail. Simple as that. Ultimately, it has nothing to do with awards, medals, and placements; it is all about putting forth maximum effort.

You have competition every day because you set such high standards for yourself that you have to go out every day and live up to that.
—Michael Jordan

CHAPTER 9

Find Your Why

I'm often asked why I do what I do. Even though my why has periodically changed over the years, my answer has for the most part been fairly consistent: "because I like it." Does that mean that the journey is easy, devoid of challenges and setbacks? Of course not. Just because I like the benefits of exercising and living a healthy life, it does not mean that it's not hard. Many athletes will confirm that practice is generally tougher than the actual event. I actually enjoy the process—go figure.

Early on, my why was following what my parents and what most of my aunts and uncles were doing athletically. It then progressed to my wanting to be more competitive at sports. Vanity then took over, so my why centered on lifting more weights, increasing my protein intake, and doing less cardio. At this point, my why has now settled on longevity and quality of life.

Find your why. It can be as superficial as wanting to wear more revealing clothing or less clothing on the beach and as serious as wanting to reverse the effects of a noncommunicable disease.

In the following text, I introduce three individuals who were gracious enough to share their stories. These individuals found their why and made lifestyle changes to be healthier, and they are now inspiring others to do the same. These three people have overcome some mental as well as physical challenges through grit, determination, and willpower. Their resilience and consistency continue to inspire me. I'm sure that their stories will do the same for you.

> **The two most important days in your life are the day you are born and the day you find out why.**
> **—Mark Twain**

Marco M.

My journey started in the month of October 2013. How I started this journey was not unusual to what our society is going through on a daily basis. It was during a dreadful physical I got the news of my being prediabetic. Not fully knowing what this meant, I was not afraid. It was not until my doctor started talking about the symptoms that I was concerned; just hearing the word *impotent* had me scared. I was a young man with a young, beautiful wife. Together, we had an active five-year-old son at the time. The next day, I was in the gym. The first couple of weeks were hard, but I was determined to finish what I started.

Along with working out once a day, I started to study this horrific disease to see how best I could get my weight down. My weight was 245 pounds at the time of my visit. Everything I studied came back to two things: diet and exercise. Right away, I started juicing my meals, eating foods with only one ingredient. The weight started to drop off fast, and I started to feel energetic.

Almost a year later, I found myself losing interest in my exercise routine, and my wife noticed it also. So she asked me to try CrossFit. I was a little skeptical about it because it was a high-intensity workout program and I didn't think I was ready for that, but I tried it anyway. I can say if it were not for the coaches and the community of CrossFit giving me the extra push I needed to continue the lifestyle that is necessary, I probably would have called it quits.

Helping people started to be a passion for me, and I found myself getting into coaching and motivating more. Four years have passed, and I am in the best shape of my life; completing a Trifecta in the Spartan Races abroad and competing in fitness competitions are some of my accomplishments. Finally, I can say if you follow the process and remain disciplined, you will see results as you live a healthier lifestyle.

> **I believe that the greatest gift you can give your family and the world is a healthy you.**
> —Joyce Meyer

Karla K.

Shortly into my freshman year of college, I fell into a pattern of mindless eating, and even though I was not exercising, I was able to keep my weight under control, or so I thought. Each year, I gained more weight, yet I never saw it necessary to make exercise a daily ritual. Despite not working out, I always admired those who did, particularly my roommate and classmate.

Moving back to The Bahamas, I got a job that had me extremely busy and required constant travel. This involved eating out a lot more than my waistline needed, and combined with high levels of stress, my health was in jeopardy. In 2012, my ankles were constantly swelling, causing so much pain and distress that I finally decided to try yet another doctor to get results.

The biggest shock came when I went on the scale and was told my weight, which had ballooned over 220 pounds and, based on my height and my body mass index, had placed me in the obese category. I was so upset with hearing this that I found myself crying in my car the entire drive home. The doctor explained that I needed to get my weight under control because my health was in serious danger. She suggested that I see a nutritionist, which I did, and also begin exercising. I began cleaning up my diet, but I struggled implementing exercise until my coworker invited me to join an exercise class.

On the first day of the class, I was so out of shape I vomited after five times up a flight of sixty-five steps. The instructor was encouraging and made an extremely embarrassing moment almost comfortable. The process was not easy, but I was committed to changing my life.

I set a goal with my coach to run a 5K race for January 2013 in honor of a friend who died of breast cancer. Preparing for the race and running it stripped me to the core. I focused on my strengths and weaknesses, and bit by bit, my life started to change. I crossed the finish line and committed myself to never allowing my health to fail. That commitment made me cross many more finish lines.

I can't change the direction of the wind, but I can adjust my sails to always reach my destination.
—Jimmy Dean

Kimwood M.

Twenty years ago, the jaws of life were used to cut me out of a wreckage—my right ear torn in three, the right side of my face sliced open, deep cuts in my neck, my seatbelt ripped through my left shoulder, and my right leg crushed and barely hanging on by the skin. I spent two full months in hospital, went through thirteen reconstructive surgeries, external followed by internal fixations, a bone graft, a muscle graft, a skin graft, and pulsed electromagnetic therapy.

The night of the accident, I was rushed to the ER. I went into toxic shock as my body rejected the steel drilled into the bone of my lower leg, and I ended up in the ICU. I was given two options by doctors: (1) cut my right leg off and get fitted for a prosthetic or (2) live in pain and barely be mobile for the rest of my life. Some doctors wanted to give up, saying there was little to no chance I could use the leg again, while others would not even attempt to save it. I created a third option—overcome the odds and prove to them that the human spirit can achieve more than medical science ever could realize.

I left the hospital in a wheelchair against doctors' orders. I eventually started using crutches for a little over a year while completing physiotherapy. I struggled with depression, pain, discomfort, and opioid addiction, but I never gave up.

Today, twenty years later, I'm living a normal, active, fun-filled, mostly pain-free life. The leg they wanted to cut off is an inch shorter than the other; has fused bones, causing limited and sometimes painful mobility in the ankle and knee; and has helped me cross numerous finish lines in races, including a full marathon. I did what only 1 percent of the world has ever done on a leg they said I would never be able to use fully again. But God … I am thankful that I survived the wreck and that God used it to prove His awesome power and make me who I am today.

My belief is stronger than your doubt.
—Dwyane Wade

It is important to find your why; your why is the spark that ignites the flame. I found that in addition to finding your why, it is equally important to attach your why to a who. The who will fan your why flame into an inextinguishable inferno. As your why changes, your who may or may not change, and vice versa. In my case, as my why changed, so did my who. My who evolved from my family (parents and their siblings) to my competitors, to me, and now to my family (my wife and kids). In the preceding stories, a visit with a doctor provided the why for all three individuals to embark on their fitness journeys. However, their whos varied drastically. Marco's who was his wife and young son, Karla's who was herself, and Kimwood's who were the doctors (naysayers or doubters). Attach your why to a who.

CHAPTER 10

Exceeding Expectations

When you set the bar so high for yourself, it is hard to surpass your expectations. However, it is easier to exceed other people's expectations when you set the bar higher than they set it for you. It still amazes me how low people tend to set the bar for me. I thought that all my past successes and efforts would give me some credit and give those around me confidence that I will surpass most if not all obstacles that cross my path. Yet there are times when those closest to me still doubt my ability, my drive, or my mindset. Honestly, the doubt may stem from concern and care rather than a lack of confidence, but I take it all the same. When you ask me, "Are you sure?" that says to me that *you* are not sure about me. Well, that just gives me another opportunity to prove you wrong and excel beyond that bar that you unknowingly set too low for me.

After the leg injury, there was surgery, then rehabilitation. After I completed all the rehabilitation, I was to compete in the Spartan Beast. I already had my head wrapped around what I needed to do to get me ready. When I spoke with the surgeon, I was told I should be fine. When I spoke with my physiotherapist, I was told I should be fine. So if the experts said that I was good to go, then that meant I was good to go.

I did not understand why those closest to me doubted that I could compete in the Spartan Beast. *Yes, I understand I had a major injury less than six months ago. Yes, I understand that I had a major surgery less than six months ago. Yes, I understand that I am fresh out of rehab. But they told me that I will be fine. I believe that I will be fine. Why, then, would you doubt my capability?* I thought. I appreciated the concern for my well-being and the natural fear of potential reinjury, but had I not proven myself in the past?

Rarely do I take irresponsible risks when it comes to my body. I will not partake in something that I have not adequately prepared for and that has the potential of hurting me. Pride will not override logic in that case. However, if I know that I put in the required work and did all the necessary effort, then logic overrides fear. Therefore, if I put in the work, I get the results.

The expectations of life depend upon diligence; the mechanic that would perfect his work must first sharpen his tools.
—Confucius

The value of preparation cannot be overstated. The work that goes on in the dark is vital. People do not see the hours in the gym, or the hours of recovery; all they see are the successes. The reason I do not exceed my expectations is because I am my own toughest critic. The reality of the situation is that the only person who has to believe is you. You will have doubters, haters, and those who are genuinely concerned, but you have to believe in yourself and in your ability and go after your goal.

The challenge truly is when we do not wholeheartedly believe in ourselves. This causes us to set unrealistic goals that we may more than likely fail to reach because they are outside our capability but they sounded good to say. An easy example of this is drastic weight loss in an unrealistic time frame. Whereas losing fifty pounds over time is plausible, losing fifty pounds in two weeks just in time for a wedding is unrealistic. Now, you can lose fifty pounds in a year, but you have to be willing to put in that consistent work and effort in your diet and exercise. If you do not put in the work, you do not get the results. Simple! You must hold yourself accountable and not stop.

When I did therapy, it was rough. I was not able to bend my leg on my own. I wanted to stop. But I had goals and I had to push through the pain. We must set the course, do what needs to be done, and put in the work. We tend to run away from the things that are uncomfortable or difficult or ugly. We must remember pain over pleasure, consistency over silence, faith over fear. We have the choice. Do we choose the temporary pleasure, not getting up early, not putting in the extra rep, or not sacrificing for the long-term reward? We are always faced with a choice. But the small choices we make daily have a long-term impact on our journeys.

**Whether you believe you can do
a thing or not, you are right.
—Henry Ford**

Come to think of it, most people doubted my full rehabilitation and my readiness to compete in the Spartan Beast. Those who did believe did so with statements of "I just want you to be careful," "What did the doctor say?" and "You sure you aren't going to reinjure yourself?" And I am sure it came out of love, but it was doubt nonetheless. However, the doubt on the outside was not stronger than the confidence I had on the inside. I had already convinced myself that I was going to be able to do the Spartan Beast. The only question I had was in what state I would be once I finished. And that is where the training and conditioning came in. I knew the key areas I needed to focus on and the key obstacles I had had issues within the other races. Therefore, it was time to prepare.

In my mind, I had already envisioned my success; it was just time to show those who doubted me, whether intentionally or unintentionally, what I already knew. I realize now that life is the same way. We have this thing inside us that we need to manifest, but those around us cannot appreciate that vision. It is our job to prepare and work on it when no one is around. We need to develop it when it is hard and push through when it seems hopeless, all while still holding on to the confidence that we can manifest this goal. So when you hear those around you, whether loved ones or haters, doubting you, understand that you are going in the right direction and this will transform you. It is your job to bring to fruition the accomplishments that you have already achieved in your mind. Set your goals, line them up, and knock them down. Always remember your voice is the loudest cheerleader and the loudest critic, and your success or failure depends on what that voice dictates.

CHAPTER 11

Pain over Regret

When you are at the crossroads of progress, you are oftentimes presented with simple choices. Succeed or fail? Stop or go? Feel pain or have regret? What are you going to choose when it is your turn? How are you going to tell your stories of heartache and pain? Every time I face that issue, I am choosing to push on. I am choosing to survive. I will not give up. Even if I keep falling down, I will keep getting back up. Even if I might not reach the top, you can tell sweet Jesus that I'm going to try. Nothing beats failure more than effort. We tend to fail not due to the circumstances we face but due to how we feel about the circumstances. Difficulties, pains, and hardships are all factors that are associated with the accent of success.

We must all suffer one of two things: the pain of discipline or the pain of regret or disappointment.
—Jim Rohn

Everything boils down to choice. When I injured my leg, I could have chosen to not complete the Trifecta. I could have also chosen to take it easy and stop pushing myself. However, that is not in my nature. I had a plan to complete the race, and this injury did not stop it, nor did it delay it; it was simply a detour on my way to my goal. I have learned that this is how life is. The more we want something, the harder it is to achieve. It is said that "if it comes easy, it is not worth it." I look at this from a biblical perspective: the path to death is wide and open, but the path to life is narrow and winding. To add to that, the path to mediocrity is easy and pain-free with no blockage. The path to greatness, however, is full of pain, sacrifice, and challenges.

We must understand that we need not give up. Stopping will impact not only our journey but the journey of others who are either depending on our success or observing our success. Who is watching you, and who else do your decisions impact? Through this injury, I learned even more how many eyes are on my journey. Even still, the confidence from others is not where it should be. All this says to me is there is more to be done. I am not on a path to prove all my naysayers wrong. I am on a path to encourage those whom I come into contact with to strive for more.

I want people to look at my journey and be inspired. I want them to see someone who never gave up. I want them to see someone who believed in himself when no one else did. I want them to see someone who created goals, lined them up, knocked them down, and started afresh. I have centered my life on choice, and I choose to be great. I will always prefer the pain of discipline over the pain of regret.

It is my intent to share my story and dare others to be better. Your being better than me will not be based on the fact that I did not accomplish all that I wanted or I missed out on the chance to live an awesome life. I want to dare you to be better than me and top what I have done. I think it is my job to set the bar higher than my parents did for me. Those who come after me will have greatness in their path simply because what I did ensured that they had greatness in their past.

Pain is temporary. Quitting lasts forever.
—Lance Armstrong

I read a post that stood out to me: "Remember that guy that quit? Neither does anybody else." While you may not intend to be world renowned, it would be nice to be remembered for something positive. I believe that if you live a life and no one remembers you, then it is a wasted life. It is wasted simply because you did not make an impact on another person. That means that you did not make use of the thing that you were given.

I feel the same way about persevering. Pain is just a test to see how bad you want something. Pain is also a qualifier for the depth of your growth. Last, pain is a detractor of false goals. If you want something, you go get it. Sometimes, it is as simple as that. The process of getting it is hard. But you cannot stop. You cannot give up. You must continue to make strides; whether you walk, crawl, or fall forward, you must continue to push on.

With my injury, I was in many tough situations; but I had already committed that I would accomplish what I set out to do. I did not put in all those hours of preparation to stop. I did not sacrifice all my time and effort to stop. I did not bring myself this far to stop. We know what our limits are; we know what our pain threshold is. I am not suggesting that you be reckless and unrealistic. I am simply saying take the blinders off your vision and take the training wheels off your vehicle. Stop holding yourself back, stop hiding from your greatness, and embrace it. Why not live the best version of you every day? Why not create the best version of your life right now? Why not be the person on the outside who you are in the inside and be happy?

Stop settling for a life that you do not want, and push through that pain. You may not have a torn muscle, but you may have a financial setback that you can rehab from and push through. You may not have a cramp in the last leg of a race, but you may have a setback in your career that you need to push through. You may not have an event to train for, but you may have a goal that seemed plausible when you set it but now, closer to time, seems more and more difficult; you need to push through. We all have pain, but the pain is not meant to last forever. We all may experience some level of regret, but that will be a choice. You must constantly choose to overcome, persevere, and push forward because pain can be forgotten, whereas regret will constantly remind you of what could have been.

CHAPTER 12

This Is Sparta

I woke up feeling great. Well rested. I was energized. I was ready! And then I went outside. It was raining, and it was cold. It was cold not just because I was from The Bahamas and accustomed to a warmer climate but because it was, as we say in the Bahamian vernacular, *cold cold*. The hotel was a substantial distance from the race site; therefore, I hoped it wasn't raining or as cold at the race site.

It rained consistently on the way to the race, which gave me little hope that the race was going to be under the shining Florida sun. So I had to get my mind right to compete in this cold. I simply reminded myself that everyone would be racing under the same conditions. In addition, I reread a text communication from the day before between one of my closest friends and me. The following is the conversation between Big Bucks Bowe (BBB) and myself:

BBB: How your preparations coming?

Me: Away now. Driving up.

BBB: Yeah I figured. Body and legs feeling ok? And mind lol.

Me: Mind playing tricks with the leg.

BBB: You Gatta follow your own motto ironically "Get Ya Mind Right"

Me: The chiropractor, surgeon and physiotherapist say it strong enough and I don't need a brace.

BBB: You gat that buddy. Just come off the nerves. If anyone in the world I gat confidence in doing stuff like that it's you buddy. You is Superman to me.

Me: Thanks bro.

BBB: Everyone is reference you when it comes to guys determination, not giving up and going above and beyond. Me, Champ, Arch. Everybody. Just from how Robbie is hear us talk about you on the court. One time we was losing, I say boy Robbie I tired and in pain. Robbie say "forget dat Donovan say tiredness and pain in ya MIND!!! Now suck it up."

Me: Dude, you have me ready to go do something now. Appreciate the talk bro!

BBB: Therefore, man it up but with sense. You een worrying about position, you coming off an injury so you just trying to finish and finish good that's all.

Me: Correct.

Just what the doctor ordered.

**Iron sharpens iron, so a friend sharpens a friend.
—Proverbs 27:17**

So now, I made my way to the race site. It was cold; however, it was time to loosen up and get ready to make things happen. In true Spartan Race fashion, one needs to climb over a wall to get to the starting line. Then there's the traditional Spartan start, unlike a traditional race start, where the announcer asks for quiet and then says, "Ready, set, go." Spartan Races start with a series of statements in question form that require the participants (Spartan Warriors) to confirm their commitment to complete the task at hand with a response of "Aroo." Then finally, after the "Aroo, aroo, aroo," I was off—gingerly, of course.

After moving slowly over the hay walls, I took time maneuvering the overwalls (a wall ranging from three to eight feet). I basically used all upper body to power up because I really didn't have the lift and jumping ability in my legs (not that I ever was a high flyer). As opposed to in my previous encounters with this obstacle, where I jumped, I allowed my hands to vault me over, and I kept it moving. Then, I softly ushered myself down one leg at a time.

To my surprise, I didn't make it over one overwall on my first attempt. At this point, I remember thinking to myself, *I een know about this leg ting. This is going to be rough.* Then it was off to once again slowly move through the over-under-through (O-U-T). Disclaimer: I took all obstacles slowly with careful takeoffs and landings.

The jog from the O-U-T to the culverts was mucky. So now I had to concern myself with activating my stabilizing muscles. After more mud, it was time to walk through some cold water, and then over the hurdles to the longest stretch of barbed wire I've ever seen. For speed, I normally do the rolling technique through this obstacle. However, the barbed wire was not as low as in previous races, so I just sort of dragged my way through using my forearm, thigh, and hip. This allowed me and other participants to have a dialogue about other races we had done and more. (I told you the stretch of barbed wire was long.)

Now off to the bucket brigade, which went really well. I had been able to spend a lot of time in the gym working on my strength training, particularly my upper-body and lower-back strength; I had made dead lifts part of my training regimen. Up and over the eight-foot wall, then it was off to the bender. Once again, I powered through with my two-inch vertical and came over the bars, which were slippery when it came to footing; therefore, I took extreme caution. I really couldn't jump down, so it was a slow, careful trek to the bottom.

Off to the races again, and then, I approached the tyro, which was awesome. While the other obstacles up to this point of the race were not new to me, this one was. So I had no experience on the best way to succeed at this discipline. I saw some of the race participants on top of the rope maneuvering like Special Forces. That wasn't going to work for me because it looked as if it required too much balance and put unnecessary pressure on the genital area. I then noticed two different ways persons were performing the underneath technique. Some were crawling like monkeys (the best way I can describe it), pulling and putting one hand over the other while their feet were doing the same thing. That way just seemed to have too many moving parts. The other way I observed was some people simply crossed their legs on the rope and just pulled their way across the rope. I understood the potential for rope burn on my legs from this technique; however, I was confident that I had put in enough upper-body work to successfully pull myself across, and I was wearing long tights to minimize rope burn. So I took the underneath approach, hooked my feet, and started to pull, pull, pull, pull, pull, pull, pull, pull, pull. I looked for the bell, and then, I pulled some more and rang that bell. I felt as if I were going a hundred miles an hour.

Feeling really energized, now I was off to the plate drag. I normally executed this obstacle from more of a squat position; however, my surgically prepared leg made that difficult. So I sat and simulated a seated cable row as if I were in the gym. It was time to get up and to take the plate back to the starting point. This was really a challenge for me. The bending and the use of my lower body made it not as easy as normal.

Now, I was off and running toward an obstacle that had eluded me in the past—the twister. In the past, I had gotten so close and then fallen short at the end. I knew that I had not only put in the proper upper-body training as it related to my upper-back strength but also focused on improving my grip strength. So now, I was ready, I thought. The twister was somewhere between miles 5 and 6. I felt strong on the apparatus as I started and felt good midway through. Now, I was controlling my emotions, not wanting to count my eggs before they hatched. I made it to the end and rang that bell harder than any other bell that I had ever rung. After I landed on one leg, fell, and rolled, I got up and gave the biggest high-five to one of the volunteers.

Running through more muck, but not caring at this point, I was about halfway through the race when I conquered an obstacle I had failed at twice before, and I was feeling great. Now off to the log carry, and I did that with relative ease. (FYI: All logs are not created equal. Find that "light" one. LOL.) Once I passed the log off, I made my way to the Z walls. I battled through that but slipped off right at the end. This meant my first set of burpees. Then on to the stairway around mile 7.

Going to mile 8, my calves started to cramp up, and my hips started to cramp up. Right before I approached the approximate ten-foot obstacle, I saw someone fall from it because they got a cramp in their calf. I did my half-inch vertical at this point and made it up and over. Off to the first sandbag carry, which took me through some mud and cold water. The fireman's log carry was a breeze. Then off to the inverted wall.

The monkey bars were next. My grip strength was on point, so I had no problem with that apparatus. I then approached the spear throw, took my time, and nailed it as normal. Obstacle 22 was the other sandbag carry. This was torture. The bags were heavier, and the mud was thick. My shoes were getting stuck in the mud. Then off to the Olympus.

I breezed through the multi-rig. The rolling mud was ridiculous. It was so thick that when I took a step, my foot came out of my shoe, which stayed in the mud. This was actually one of the toughest obstacles because the water was cold and the mud placed so much resistance on my leg as I maneuvered my way in and out of those ditches. Then, I was off to the slip wall. No problem there. By this time, I could hear people celebrating that they'd finished, and I could also see the finish line. Sadly, however, the path veered in the opposite direction of the finish line.

After the six-foot wall posed no challenge, it was time for the Atlas lift (obstacle number 28). And somewhere around mile 11, I was getting fatigued, and the bending was posing a slight problem in my right thigh, left hamstring, and both hips. What made it worse was the temperature started to drop and rain, which held up at the start of the race began to fall again. Gingerly, I went over the vertical cargo net. My energy reserves were gone, and my core body temperature was lowering at this point.

Now, I was walking toward my arch nemesis—the rope climb. I had my technique down pat, and this time, I was ready to conquer it. *Nope, not today.* The cramping in my hips made it impossible, so off to the burpee area I went. Then, I walked to the Hercules hoist—and completed that with ease—and crawled over the A frame and ended with the fire jump. And that was that. The race was done. I was happy, and I was cold—cold to the point where I was actually shivering. So it was time to get my photo taken and get to the warmth of the car.

I was so excited to have completed the race!

CHAPTER 13

The Heart of a Spartan

From completing the race, I realized that the race was not just something to do. It opened the door to more possibilities. It had seemed difficult going into it, but if there were people who completed the obstacles, then I knew that with proper training, I would be able to complete them as well. With hindsight, I can still admit that the race was difficult, but I was able to complete it. There was no particularly difficult task. Each obstacle had its own challenges, and with each challenge, I learned something specific about my body, my development, and my journey.

If you find a path with no obstacles, it probably doesn't lead anywhere.
—Frank A. Clark

With the Spartan Beast, I expected the obstacles, but that did not make going through them any easier. In life, you can see hardships coming, but it still hurts to go through them, and you have to push on. I knew I was going to face a difficult time naturally because the race is difficult. Adding to this, I was months away from surgery and fresh off rehab. But I had not come that far to be one-third short of my Trifecta because I had hurt my leg, so I pushed on. I needed to do it for me; I had set the goal earlier in the year, and I was to accomplish it. And that I did.

The craziest thing was the weather. With this race in December, it was uncomfortably cold, and given the amount of water obstacles and rain, it made it feel even colder. That showed me another life lesson: even when you prepare for the known obstacles, there a few unknown obstacles that you just cannot prepare for.

One of the main rules for the race is that every failed obstacle results in a thirty burpee penalty, and there were thirty to thirty-five obstacles. Needless to say, I could not afford to fail these obstacles. I rarely meet someone who is a fan of burpees. Can you imagine doing burpees after running twelve to fourteen miles in the cold and then having to do burpees after thirty to thirty-five obstacles? If that is not motivation to get it right the first time, then I do not know what is.

> **I will not surrender to the course.**
> **—Donovan J. Rolle Sr.**

I went into the race knowing that I would complete it. I never questioned whether I would complete the race; I had resolved to start the first leg of the Trifecta. I will not surrender to the course. But the course I am referring to is larger than the Spartan Race. The course I will not surrender to is life. In life, there will be challenges and obstacles to overcome. The quicker we learn that life is meant not to overwhelm us but to help us grow, learn, and enjoy, the quicker we maximize all our opportunities. Like with the Spartan Race, in life, we need to plan, prepare, and perform.

Once I committed to the race, I immediately went into planning mode. I had to make travel arrangements. I had to get the details of the course. I had to create a training schedule that would prepare me for the race. After the planning, I had to prepare for the event. This is when I executed all the pre-event plans I had. I had to train. I had to eat better. I had to practice. Most important, I had to be disciplined. Without preparation, planning is fruitless. But without planning, you will not perform to the best of your capabilities. Last came the performing. As with most things, you perform how you practice. Most disappointments occur when people do not put in the work prior but expect the top results. You may have a few occasions where you outperform your expectations, but normally, you get out what you put in. Therefore, we need to take this approach in life—plan, prepare, and then perform.

If you go through life with no sense of direction, you might go nowhere. You might end up somewhere that helps you or somewhere that hurts you. Ultimately, it is difficult for you to end up where you want if you do not clearly state where you want to go initially. We must be intentional about this course that we call *life*. We cannot just passively sit by and wait for it to happen. We must name what we want, prepare for it, work toward it, and then act accordingly when we get there.

You will have some unexpected injuries, obstacles, or detours on your journey as I have had on mine. In the moment, these challenges can seem to overshadow our destination. However, in these moments, if we rely on our preparation and planning, this will push us past the difficult moments. After my recovery and rehab, my planning and preparation are what gave me the confidence to perform. If I did not put in the time physically, I would not have had the mental confidence to perform.

Fitness is more than just an event. It is a mental, physical, and spiritual state that we must take on. Having the heart of a Spartan is knowing that you have set the course, have put in the work, and will perform to the best of your capabilities. This approach is the same one we need for life. It is time to take life head-on. Dare to aim for the difficult. Embrace the challenges and setbacks that will definitely come along the way. Remember these are not meant to stop you; they are meant for you to overcome. So keep on going.

CHAPTER 14

Jay All Day

I have always envied those who are able to inspire others. These people include those who have made lifestyle changes and lost massive amounts of weight, then taken it further by taking their talent to the bodybuilding and fitness stage. I'm amazed by those who intentionally missed PE in high school and now are competing in 5Ks, half marathons, and even full marathons. I'm amazed by those who had bad eating habits and are now ensuring that individuals know the importance of a balanced meal, proper portion size, and nutritional content. I'm amazed by those who were informed during a doctor's visit that they were fast approaching hypertension and well on their way to diabetes medication and are now leading daily fitness classes. They are examples of creating what you want. They are examples of never settling. They are examples of people who are out to make the best versions of themselves, day in and day out.

While I have been able to motivate a few people to make lifestyle changes for the better, still many remain untouched. Many were of the view that I could not understand their journey of pain on the road to fitness. They thought that my push was unrealistic or my mindset manufactured and not organic. They did not fully understand that the way I motivated them is the same way I motivate myself. I believe that growth and improvement are constant factors of life. I also believe that we should be the best versions of ourselves all day, every day. But for some reason, many were of the view that I was born fit and I maintain this level of fitness with little to no effort—that somehow, my maintenance and even my drive to get better and my ability to meet new challenges come easy for me. Let me assure you anything associated with my journey is not, nor has ever been, easy.

> **Success is a lousy teacher. It seduces smart people into thinking they can't lose.**
> **—Bill Gates**

On July 30, 2017, an unforeseen twist of fate provided me with the opportunity to do what I thought would forever escape me. Surely, my injury was enough of a setback that overcoming it and performing at a decent level in a timely manner would indicate my will, my determination, and, more important, my mindset ("Get ya mind right")—and not some magic pill—were the reasons for my fitness level. I always believed in the road less traveled. But also, I always believed that once I set my foot on the path, then I would do all I could to see it through.

I believe that because my nature is to not give up, people confuse my success with ease. All the things I wanted I had to work for, and work exceptionally hard for. Nothing was handed to me. Fitness was not handed to me. Success was not handed to me. Dedication was not handed to me. I had to go out and get it. And once I got it, I had to fight to keep it. What kept me going was the simple fact that someone else is always working harder or longer, and I must do my best to ensure I perform to the best of my ability day in and day out.

Do not mistake my success for lack of hardship. Look at my success as a testament to my consistency in sticking to my plan, my dedication to always give my best effort, and my focus on what I want out of my life. You can do the same thing in any area of your life. Once you are willing to put in the time, energy, and effort, you will find there are few things you will not be successful at.

The next time you admire someone for standing on the mountaintop, make sure you pay respect to the hills and valleys they had to overcome to get to that point. Also, do not be ashamed to share where you are in your journey. People need to see the authentic you every day. I am Jay all day! To me, that means I am the same person regardless of external circumstances simply because I am confident in myself, my talents, and my abilities.

When you look at people who are successful, you will find that they aren't the people who are motivated, but have consistency in their motivation.
—Arsene Wenger

Once you win the battle within, conquering your goals will become easier. Remember that your journey inspires others the same way you take inspiration from someone else's journey. Do not be ashamed or afraid to share where you are. Also, be selfless, and help others along their journeys. Whether you help them through an encouraging word, a listening ear, or any other kind of support, understand that we are in this together.

CHAPTER 15

Proper Training

Health and wellness is not just physical. Proper fitness includes having a sound body, mind, and spirit. During training, I ensure that I address all three areas. If I were to take care of just my body and neglect my mind and spirit, then my body would suffer. And the same could be said of focusing on my mind and spirit and neglecting my body. Proper training includes focus, consistency, and patience. In my rehab and after it, I grew greater patience, as I had to do all the proper steps and had to follow the planned timeline.

With training, you will encounter setbacks and delays. Even after my rehab was completed and I finished the race, I still did not feel 100 percent. The struggle was, in fact, very much real. Six months after rehabilitation, I was still experiencing challenges. In many instances, I was rarely able to move without thought and effort. Simple actions like coming down the stairs proved difficult at times. I found myself overcompensating with my good leg when I went for short runs. I was uncertain whether the difficulty was physical or mental, but I knew that I needed to further develop both my physical strength and my mental strength. I needed to continue strengthening my leg, and I needed to have mental confidence. Due to my overcompensating, I developed a discomfort in my hip joints and sharp pains in my knee on my good leg.

> **I hated every minute of training, but I said,
> "Don't quit. Suffer now and live the rest
> of your life as a champion."**
> —Muhammad Ali

I appreciate my fitness even more since my injury simply because my consistency prior to my injury aided my consistency throughout my rehabilitation. It is important to practice how we wish to perform because we never know when those habits will be tested. Those small things we take for granted, or those things that we tend to overlook, are usually building blocks that will help us overcome future obstacles.

I often questioned how I could have avoided the injury. I did all the things I was supposed to do. But the unexpected still happened. And that is a simple life lesson: no matter how much you prepare and train, there will always be obstacles and pitfalls along your journey. As the old saying goes, it is not how many times you fall down but how many times you get up. I refuse to stay down. I always aim to get back up. I train to get back up. I will get back up.

My training was not just for the next event but for the next pitfall. Proper training encompasses physical fitness as well as mental, emotional, and spiritual fitness. The physical part is the surface level that we all see. However, those other factors play a pivotal role in fitness.

Mental health is something we tend to shy away from. We avoid dealing with matters of the mind before it is too late. The diseases tend to be the outcome. For our mental fitness, we need to deal with the contributors. A major contributor to mental well-being is stress. When we allow situations that we have no control over to impact us, we get stressed, and it impacts our entire being. As the Serenity Prayer states, "Accept the things I cannot change, change the things I can, and have the wisdom to know the difference." When you let go of what you cannot control—other people, their opinions, work issues—and control things you can control—yourself, yourself-confidence, your work ethic—then you can prepare yourself to handle the stressors of the world.

Emotional health is imperative in sustaining a long and healthy life as well. Bitterness not only drives people away but also weighs us down. We must learn to let go of hurt feelings and grudges. It is said that holding a grudge against another is like drinking poison and expecting someone else to die. We must train to forgive in small situations, as this will give us experience in forgiving larger issues. Once we accept that everyone is not perfect, including us, we can understand that everyone will disappoint us to some extent. Some persons will intentionally hurt you, and others will mistakenly hurt you, but you must still forgive. Forgiveness is not for them; it is for you. When you release them from needing your forgiveness, you release yourself from holding on to that hurt. Forgiving in the small is training for forgiveness in the large. Ultimately, we must learn to forgive because we one day will be seeking forgiveness.

Last but not least is the foundation, your spiritual health. Whether you believe in one God or the power of the universe, you must acknowledge there is a source greater than you, and you must align yourself with that source. Daily training means prayer, meditation, or reflection. This involves having quiet and alone time to not only speak but also listen. Listen to what your spirit tells you. Seek the path that is laid out for you. When you are in tune with your spirit, your life will follow suit. Again, training for this starts in the small. Seek to have quiet time while things are going well, not just when things are rough. Seek reflection time while you have time in your schedule, not just when things are busy. If we make these things part of our routine when things are calm, we'll already have spiritual habits that we can fall back on when we experience our rough patches.

Doing the best at this moment puts you in the best place for the next moment.
—Oprah Winfrey

Ultimately, you must take care of your whole self—the parts that the world sees along with the parts that only you see. Too many people only focus on what the world sees, and that is evidenced by people who reach their fitness goals but are still unhappy. They place too much focus on the wrong thing and have no balance. From a fitness perspective, that is like building up your chest but neglecting your back muscles. Or, it is like developing your biceps and neglecting your triceps. Or, it is like focusing on your quadriceps without strengthening your hamstrings. Training is all about balance. Life is all about balance. If you can master balance in the small, then when life gets increasingly more difficult, you will rely on your training and reach balance in the large.

CHAPTER 16

Family First

I got my competitive nature from my father and my resilient nature from my mother. My father was a Green Beret, so fitness was part of his regimen. He also left me no room for excuses, no room for not completing a task that I set out to do.

My mother has a thirst for competition and also follows the ethos of getting the job done. Her resilience never ceases to amaze me. One example of it is at age fifty-nine, she went on a trip to the Holy Land, where she got a chance to experience the passion of Christ. She had to carry a life-size cross to the hilltop just like Christ. That was impressive by itself; but unbeknownst to her, she made the trek on a broken foot. She thought it was just swollen, but when she got back home, it was diagnosed as broken. That meant she had traveled with the cross with a broken foot and minimal aid. If that is not resilience, then I do not know what is.

What solidified my thirst for competition were my childhood memories. All throughout my childhood home, we had numerous accolades on display. We ran out of display space; therefore, only first-, second-,and third-place awards made the cut. We had no counter space for participation awards. The combination of grit and determination from my parents is something I carry throughout my life and will pass on to the next generation, not just through genetics but through demonstration.

> **The bond that links your true family is not one of blood, but of respect and joy in each other's life.**
> **—Richard Bach**

I was bred to be a beast and taught that what you start, you finish. This mindset is what led me to start my fitness family, Jay Fitness, where the motto is "Get ya mind right." As the paternal figure of this fitness family, I need to lead not only through my words but also through my lifestyle. Therefore, I practice what I preach. When it comes to will and effort, I will get the job done. What continues to motivate me to push my limits is simply my family. They give me strength to push on, and they constantly demonstrate the products of effort and hard work. I seek to be the driving force for the future generation. I want my family to draw their strength from me, the same way I draw my strength from my family.

> **Family and friendships are two of the greatest facilitators of happiness.**
> **—John C. Maxwell**

I have been blessed with a beautiful family. The connections of the Rolle–Kelly clan; my loving wife and my two pairs of twin heartbeats, London & Donovan Jr. and Jaylen & Jayden; my Jay Fitness family; and the countless other circles I am involved in make life worth living. There is no trophy that can replace my family. There is no victory that can overshadow a friendship. There is no race that is more important than furthering the love, encouragement, and positivity that have been the foundation of my life. I show my appreciation more through my actions than through my words. I believe that men should say less and do more. With that said, I will continue to demonstrate my love and appreciation to all my families and friends by being the best version of myself, showing them that they, too, can be the best versions of themselves.

CHAPTER 17

Leaving a Legacy

For me, leaving a legacy is more than just leaving behind tangible things for my friends and loved ones. It is about leaving behind an idea. Do not get me wrong; it is my job to ensure my family is taken care of financially. I also seek to add to the structure of love and support that my family has established. This will be passed down throughout my family's future generations for all to benefit. Ultimately, whenever someone remembers me, I want them to remember, "Yes, you can!" I want to leave behind not only positivity but inspiration. I want the people who come in contact with me to leave me with a better appreciation of themselves.

My objective is to bring out the best in people. I do not add anything to their makeup. I do not force any ideals upon them. I simply pull out the gems that people have hidden inside. I remove the moss of self-doubt that is covering the beautiful statue of self-worth and self-love. The can-do spirit is important. You can do anything and everything. You can! Why not you? Believe in you and do. My legacy is you can do it. Yes, *I* can. Why can't *you* do it? "Because people told me no" is not enough. You must be the catalyst of what more can be done. You must believe in yourself. Break the mold. Break the barriers. Yes, you can do it! Yes, you!

> **It is up to us to live up to the legacy that was left for us, and to leave a legacy that is worthy of our children and of future generations.**
> **—Christine Gregoire**

I was lucky to have great things left in place for me related to character, work ethic, determination, and an overall approach to life. It is important that I not only maximize what was given to me but leave something greater behind for those after me. To leave a legacy for my children, I must lead by example. "Do as I say and not as I do" was disproven a long time ago. I want them to see that they can believe and achieve anything and everything because I tried. Daddy tried to excel in academics and athletics; therefore, I am allowing them to believe they can push themselves academically and athletically. But it is bigger than that. If they choose to excel in other arenas, I hope they take my spirit of persistence and excellence and apply it to their path of choice. I want them to remember that I exposed them to more. I purposely did this so they can dream of more. The more they see, the more they can achieve.

As their father, my role is to put them in a position to see the many doors of opportunities life has to offer. I will not only show them but encourage them to pick the door that speaks to them and to walk through it with confidence and determination—they must run their own race and do what they feel they must do. I want to leave behind more than just financial security; I want to leave behind a sense of security in oneself. I do not expect people to be me. I expect them to be better. I expect them to learn from my mistakes and develop my strengths. Grit, determination, hard work, consistency, self-worth, drive, and excellence are just a few items I am passing on to them that will definitely help them tackle and conquer their own individual races.

> **My legacy is that I stayed on course …from the beginning to the end, because I believed in something inside of me.**
> **—Tina Turner**

I have my fitness family fooled. They may come to me to get fit or to lose weight or to reach any other fitness goal. But what they get from me is a positive environment, a support system, and a belief that they can do anything they want to do as long as they put the work in. They can actually do it by themselves. I only help them appreciate that there are no free lunches and there is no shortcut to accomplishing their goals. The legacy I want for my fitness family is that when they think of Jay, they think of possibility. Jay Fitness is a mindset. It is a can-do mindset that lives in a positive environment in a realm of endless possibilities. I am only the gatekeeper. This is bigger than one person. If we could get the entire world to get their minds right, imagine the impact we would have on not only this generation but future generations.

> **Carve your name on hearts, not tombstones. A legacy is etched into the minds of others and the stories they share about you.**
> **—Shannon L. Alder**

They say hard work beats talent when talent doesn't work hard. Well, I'm that hard-working talent who finishes what he starts. I will not stop because I'm tired. I will finish when I am done. I do not have more time than another person. I have the same amount of time as the other person. I have the same opportunities as the other person. I have the same talents as the other person. The biggest difference between myself and others is simple: I saw what I wanted, I went after what I wanted, and I did not stop.

There is no special formula for success. It is all about hard work, determination, belief, and vision. There are no shortcuts to the road to greatness. There are no easy paths up the mountain of self-actualization. There is no shortened version of the test of self-discipline. Simply put in the work, and accept what comes out of it. If you do not like the outcome, work harder. If you are satisfied with the outcome, teach others how to do what you did.

You will meet many friends and enemies during your journey of getting your mind right. For me, commitment, determination, and consistency are my allies; regret is my enemy. I enjoy the company of my friends, I cherish what they bring, and I do my best to honor their presence. I learn from my enemies. I do my endeavor best to avoid spending any time in their company. I have gotten my mind right, and I continue to maintain it every day. I teach others to do the same not just through my words but through my actions. Quite frankly, I am the beast that gets the job done!